My Animal Garden
Adult Coloring Book Stress Relieving Designs

Illustrations hand drawn by Mrs. Lynnette Jones
Dedication: For all the people who love me.
Love Always, Lynnette

Butterflies, Bunnies and Bears, Oh My. My Animal Garden is a mix of cute animals and flowers that Lynnette enjoys drawing. Imagine looking out your window into a garden and finding the animals on these coloring pages. Lynnette has traveled to many National Parks in the United States to see the wild animals in their natural habitat. She has hand drawn for you the wild horses that live at Assateague Island National Park in Maryland, wild rabbits from Joshua Tree National Park in California, wild black bears living at Sequoia National Park in California, grizzly bears living in Denali National Park Alaska, wild deer living at Kings Canyon National Park in California, birds, bunnies and pet lambs from her dad's farm in Iowa. Each hand drawn page has a hidden ladybug for you to find and color.

Some Bunny Loves You

www.HotPinkStudio.me

Have patience and tolerance.

www.HotPinkStudio.me

You have the Strength of an Elephant

www.HotPinkStudio.me

I Love You Beary Much

You Belong were You Feel Free

www.HotPinkStudio.me

Collect Memories not Things

www.HotPinkStudio.me

One must be kind,
as every bunny is fighting a battle.

www.HotPinkStudio.me

Just Keep Breathin
everything will be ok

www.HotPinkStudio.me

Everything is hard before it is easy.

Don't tell people your dream,
Show Them.

It always seems impossible
until it is done.

Dive into silence then take action

Never think of failure at all, for as you think now, that is what you will get.

www.HotPinkStudio.me

Relationships are based on giving.

www.HotPinkStudio.me

Nature knows best how to organise

See the job, do the job,
stay out of the misery.

www.HotPinkStudio.me

Don't compare yourself to others.

Let us Love, be Loving and spread Love around us.

www.HotPinkStudio.me

Always Choose Happiness

www.HotPinkStudio.me

Pick something great to do and do it

www.HotPinkStudio.me

What you think you become

www.HotPinkStudio.me

Take one hop forward each day
to your dreams

The answers are found in silence

Speak Truth to Power

www.HotPinkStudio.me

Be simple, be kind, stay rested

No one on this green eart is smarter than you.
You can learn to do anything you want to in life.

www.HotPinkStudio.me

More support of nature comes from being happy

www.HotPinkStudio.me

Success is through happiness

www.HotPinkStudio.me

Go for what you really want

www.HotPinkStudio.me

Keep your desire turning back within and be patient

www.HotPinkStudio.me

www.HotPinkStudio.me

www.HotPinkStudio.me

www.HotPinkStudio.me

www.HotPinkStudio.me

www.HotPinkStudio.me

www.HotPinkStudio.me

www.HotPinkStudio.me

www.HotPinkStudio.me

www.HotPinkStudio.me

www.HotPinkStudio.me

www.HotPinkStudio.me

www.HotPinkStudio.me

www.HotPinkStudio.me

www.HotPinkStudio.me

www.HotPinkStudio.me

www.HotPinkStudio.me

www.HotPinkStudio.me

www.HotPinkStudio.me

www.HotPinkStudio.me